Following Directions

Grades 1-2

Written by
Linda Schwartz

Illustrated by
Mark Mason

Editor: Kelly Scott
Illustrator: Mark Mason
Cover artist: Kimberly Schamber
Designer: Eric Larson, Studio E Books
Cover Designer: Barbara Peterson
Art Director: Tom Cochrane
Project Director: Linda Schwartz

How To Use This Book

The activities in this book will give your students practice and competence in following written directions, step-by-step directions, and oral directions. In addition to the worksheets, the only supplies needed are pencils and crayons. The first section of the book contains written directions for your students to follow. In the second section, written step-by-step directions and illustrations instruct students to draw simple pictures. In the third section, you read a set of directions to your students while they listen and do the work on their activity sheets. Pages in the book may be used in any order.

Contents

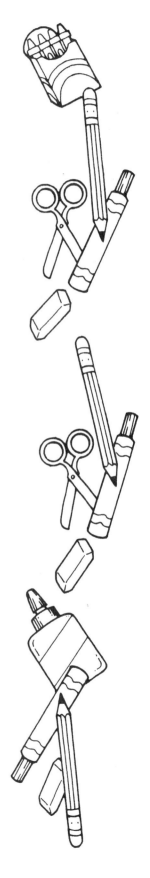

Contents (continued)

Following Written Directions

Dot-to-Dot Pet

Pedro just got a new pet. To find out what kind it is, connect the dots in ABC order. Begin with the letter **A** and end with the letter **Z**.

What kind of pet did Pedro get? _____

Following Directions • 1–2   ©2004 Creative Teaching Press

Dot-to-Dot Creature

What kind of creature is this? To find out, connect the dots in ABC order.
Begin with the letter **A** and end with the letter **Z**.

The creature is a(n) _____ .

Who's in the Zoo?

Who's in the zoo? To find out, connect the dots by counting.
Begin with the number **1** and end with the number **25**.

The animal in the zoo is a(n) _____ .

Following Directions • 1–2   ©2004 Creative Teaching Press

The Surprise Package

What's inside the package? To find out, connect the dots by counting.
Begin with the number **1** and end with the number **25**.

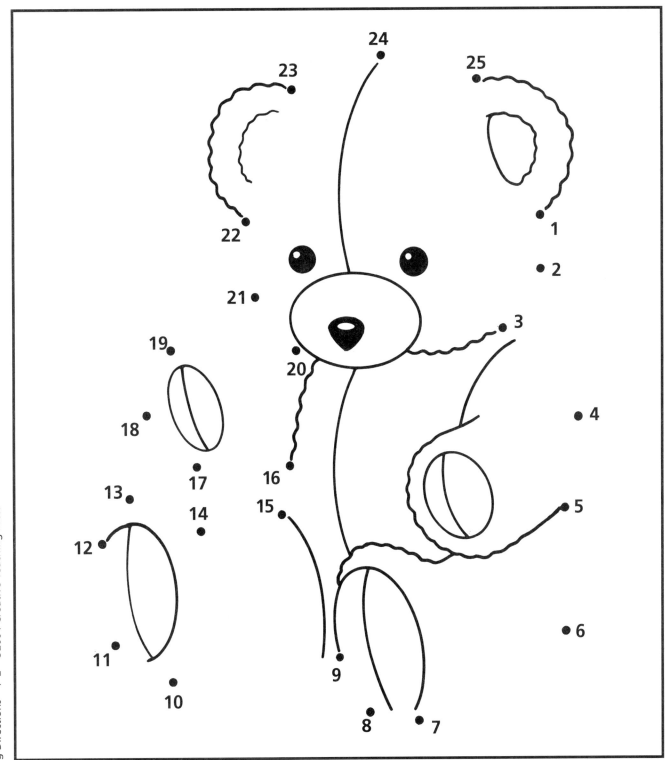

Inside the package is a(n) _____ .

Color the Sweaters

Follow the directions to color these sweaters.

1. Color the sweater with two pockets blue.
2. Color the sweater with the hood green.
3. Color the sweater with the zipper pink.
4. Color the sweater with three buttons brown.
5. Color the sweater with stripes red and orange.
6. Color the sweater with a collar black.

Following Directions • 1–2 ©2004 Creative Teaching Press

Big on Bugs

Follow the directions to color these bugs.

1. Color the bug on the rock red.
2. Color the flying bug purple.
3. Color the bug on the flower yellow and red.
4. Color the bug in the bush orange.
5. Color the smallest bug pink.
6. Color the twin bugs blue.
7. Color the bug on the ground green.
8. Color the largest bug brown.

Colorful Fish

Follow the directions to color the fish.

1. Color the fish with the longest tail yellow.
2. Color the fish with the most fins purple.
3. Color the fish swimming closest to the sand green.
4. Color the fish with stripes orange.
5. Color the fish with dots brown.
6. Color the smallest fish pink.
7. Color the fish closest to the plant blue.
8. Color the fish in the upper right-hand corner red.

Following Directions • 1–2 ©2004 Creative Teaching Press

Color the Clown

Follow the directions to color the clown.

1. Color the clown's nose purple.
2. Color the clown's eyes blue.
3. Color the ruffle pink.
4. Color the clown's mouth red.
5. Color the clown's hair orange.
6. Draw two green stripes on the top pom-pom on the clown's hat.
7. Draw three yellow triangles on the middle pom-pom.
8. Draw four small red circles on the bottom pom-pom.

Following Directions • 1–2 ©2004 Creative Teaching Press

Riddle Time #1

"Why is a giraffe the cheapest pet to feed?"

To find the answer to the riddle, follow the directions below.
Write the words on the lines on page 15.

Write the word **feed** on line #3.

Write the word **little** on line #6.

Write the word **you** on line #2.

Write the word **goes** on line #7.

Write the word **it** on line #4.

Write the word **way** on line #10.

Write the word **When** on line #1.

Write the word **a** on line #5 and on line #8.

Write the word **long** on line #9.

Following Directions • 1–2 ©2004 Creative Teaching Press

Riddle Time #1

To find the answer to the riddle, write the words from page 14 on the lines below.

Then read the answer going down the page.

1. _____

2. _____

3. _____

4. _____

5. _____

6. _____

7. _____

8. _____

9. _____

10. _____

Riddle Time #2

"Why didn't the pilot allow the elephant on the airplane?"

To find the answer to the riddle, follow the directions below.
Write the words on the lines on page 17.

Write the word **to** on line #6.

Write the word **was** on line #3.

Write the word **the** on line #9.

Write the word **big** on line #5.

Write the word **seat** on line #10.

Write the word **fit** on line #7.

Write the word **His** on line #1.

Write the word **too** on line #4.

Write the word **trunk** on line #2.

Write the word **under** on line #8.

Following Directions • 1–2 ©2004 Creative Teaching Press

Riddle Time #2

To find the answer to the riddle, write the words from page 16 on the lines below.

Then read the answer going down the page.

1. _____

2. _____

3. _____

4. _____

5. _____

6. _____

7. _____

8. _____

9. _____

10. _____

Birthday Party Bears

Follow the directions and color the bears on page 19.
Put an X in the box in front of each direction
when you have done what it says.

☐ 1. Color the left bear's tie green.

☐ 2. Color the right bear's shirt purple.

☐ 3. Color the left bear's gift yellow.

☐ 4. Color the right bear's bow tie brown.

☐ 5. Color the left bear's hat orange.

☐ 6. Color the left bear's pants blue.

☐ 7. Color the right bear's shoes purple.

☐ 8. Draw red stripes on the right bear's pants.

Following Directions • 1–2 ©2004 Creative Teaching Press

Birthday Party Bears

Color the bears using the directions on page 18.

Name: _____

Race Cars in a Row

Follow directions and color the race cars on page 21.
Put an X in the box in front of each direction
when you have done what it says.

☐ 1. Color the numbers on all of the car doors yellow.

☐ 2. Color the tires on all of the cars black.
    Leave the centers white.

☐ 3. Color car number 5 blue.

☐ 4. Color car number 6 yellow.

☐ 5. Color car number 1 red.

☐ 6. Color car number 3 green.

☐ 7. Color car number 2 purple.

☐ 8. Color car number 4 orange.

Following Directions • 1–2   ©2004 Creative Teaching Press

Race Cars in a Row

Color the race cars using the directions on page 20.

Hidden Flower

A flower is hidden in this picture. To find it, follow these directions.

1. Color all the shapes with **G** green.
2. Color all the shapes with **B** blue.
3. Color all the shapes with **Y** yellow.
4. Color all the shapes with **R** red.

Following Directions • 1–2   ©2004 Creative Teaching Press

Hidden Bird

A bird is hidden in this picture. To find it, follow these directions.

1. Color all the shapes with **G** green.
2. Color all the shapes with **B** blue.
3. Color all the shapes with **Y** yellow.
4. Color all the shapes with **R** red.

Hidden Dinosaur

A dinosaur is hidden in this picture. To find it, follow these directions.

1. Color all the shapes with **G** green.
2. Color all the shapes with **B** blue.
3. Color all the shapes with **Y** yellow.
4. Color all the shapes with **R** red.

Following Directions • 1–2   ©2004 Creative Teaching Press

The Candy Store

Find the gumdrops. Color three gumdrops purple and three gumdrops yellow.

Find the jelly beans. Color five jelly beans black and four jelly beans green.

Find the gumballs. Color seven gumballs blue and three gumballs red.

Find the candy canes. Color the stripes on the candy canes red. Leave the rest of each candy cane white.

Find the candy corn. Leave the tip of each piece of candy corn white. Color the middle of each piece of candy corn yellow. Color the big end orange.

Following Directions • 1–2 ©2004 Creative Teaching Press

Jake's Lost!

Jake followed Mike to school, and now Jake is lost!
Follow directions to help the dog find his way back home.

Use the map on page 27, and draw a path with your pencil or crayon.

1. Find the school in the upper left-hand corner.

2. Take Oak Avenue east to Elm Street. Turn south on Elm Street.

3. Take Elm Street to The Doggie Diner.

4. From The Doggie Diner, take Maple Lane west to Palm Park.

5. Leave Palm Park and go south on Cypress Street to the fire station.

6. Now go east on Walnut Avenue to home.

7. Draw a bone in front of the house as a treat.

Following Directions • 1–2 ©2004 Creative Teaching Press

Jake's Lost!

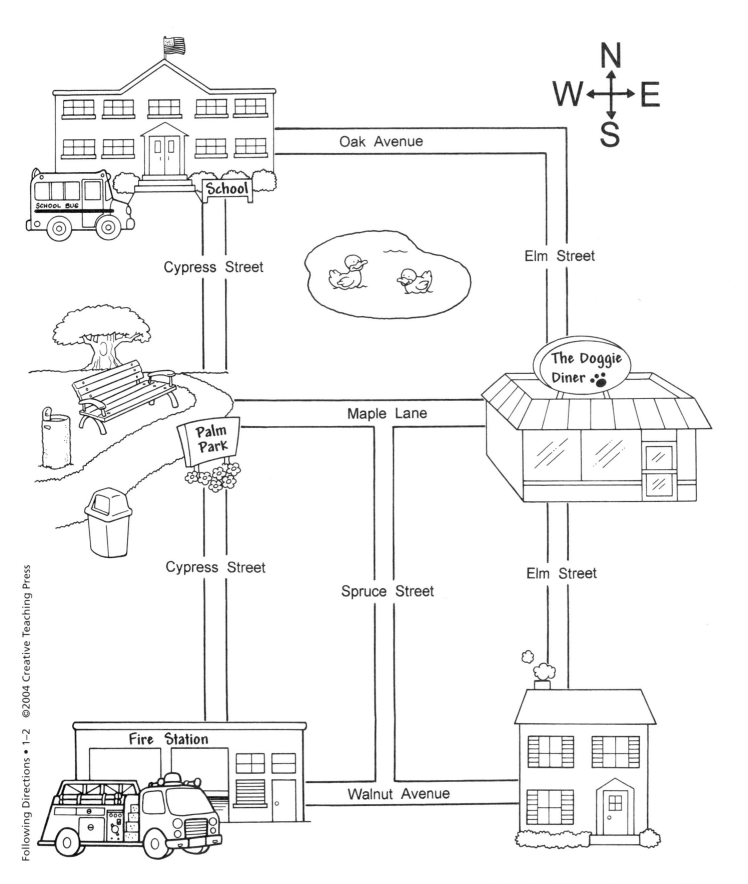

Crack the Code

Use the code to find the secret message.
Write a letter for each picture symbol. The first one has been done for you.

A	D	E	H	P	V	Y
△	◯	☐	♡	◇	☆	◑

H ___ ___ ___ ___

___

___ ___ ___ ___ ___

___ ___ ___ !

Following Directions • 1–2   ©2004 Creative Teaching Press

Following
Step-by-Step Directions
To Draw a Picture

Draw a Pig

#1

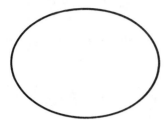

Draw an oval for the
body of the pig.

#2

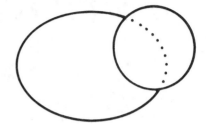

Add a circle for the head.
Erase the dotted line.

#3

Add ears and a nose.
Erase the dotted line.

#4

Add eyes, a mouth, legs,
and a curly tail.

Draw your pig here. Give your pig an apple to eat.

Following Directions • 1–2   ©2004 Creative Teaching Press

Name: _____

Draw a Submarine

#1
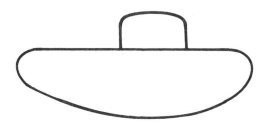
Draw the body of the submarine.

#2
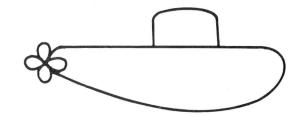
Add a propeller.

#3
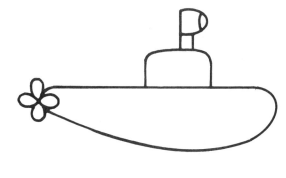
Add a periscope.

#4
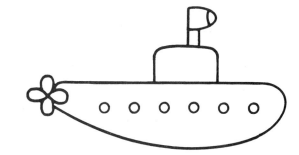
Add six portholes on the side of the submarine.

Draw your submarine here. Add some fish to your picture.

Draw a Cow

#1

Draw the body of the cow.

#2

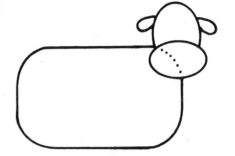

Draw the head and ears.
Erase the dotted line.

#3

Add horns, eyes, a nose, and a mouth.
Draw four legs.

#4

Draw hooves on each leg, and add a tail.
Add spots to the cow's body.

Draw your cow here. Draw grass for your cow to eat.

Following Directions • 1–2   ©2004 Creative Teaching Press

Draw a Turtle

#1

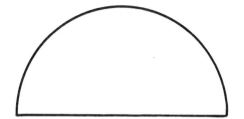

Draw the top part
of the turtle's shell.

#2

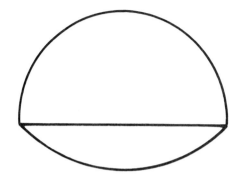

Draw the bottom part
of the turtle's shell.

#3

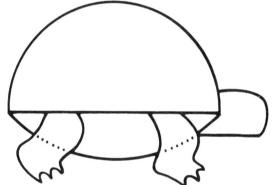

Draw the turtle's head and legs.
Erase the dotted lines.

#4

Add a mouth, an eye, and a tail.
Draw lines on the turtle's shell.

Draw your turtle here. Draw some strawberries for your turtle to eat.

Following Directions • 1–2   ©2004 Creative Teaching Press

Draw an Alligator

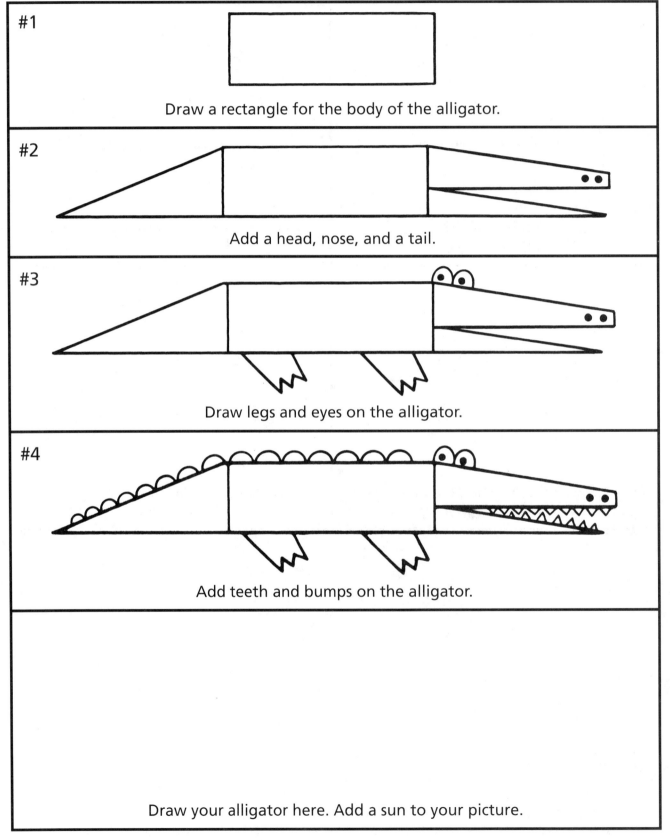

#1

Draw a rectangle for the body of the alligator.

#2

Add a head, nose, and a tail.

#3

Draw legs and eyes on the alligator.

#4

Add teeth and bumps on the alligator.

Draw your alligator here. Add a sun to your picture.

Following Directions • 1–2 ©2004 Creative Teaching Press

Draw an Owl

#1

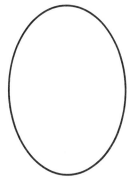

Draw a large oval for the
body of the owl.

#2

Draw a wavy line for the owl's head.
Add the wings.

#3

Draw eyes and a beak on the owl's head.
Add wavy lines for the owl's feathers.

#4

Draw ears, feet, and a branch
for the owl to perch on.

Draw your owl here. Add a moon to your picture.

Name: _____

Draw a Kangaroo

#1

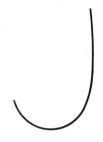

Draw a letter "J."

#2

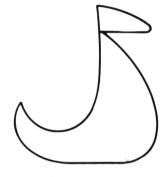

Draw the head, body,
and tail of the kangaroo.

#3

Draw the kangaroo's arm, front leg,
and foot. Erase the dotted line.

#4

Draw ears, an eye, a nose,
and a pouch.

Draw your kangaroo here.

Draw the head of a joey
(a baby kangaroo) peeking
out of your kangaroo's pouch.

Following Directions • 1–2   ©2004 Creative Teaching Press

Draw a Kitten

#1

Draw the bottom half of a circle
for the kitten's body.

#2

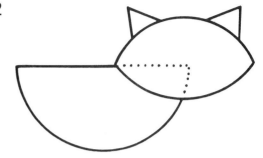

Draw the head and ears.
Erase the dotted lines.

#3

Add four legs and a tail. Draw a face on
the kitten, and add stripes to the body.

#4

Draw eyes, a nose, a mouth, and
whiskers. Draw claws on the kitten's feet.

Draw your kitten here. Add a ball of yarn for your kitten to play with.

Following Directions • 1–2 ©2004 Creative Teaching Press

Draw a Clown

#1

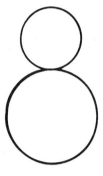

Draw a large circle with a smaller circle on top.

#2

Add arms, hands, and legs.

#3

Draw a face. Add buttons, pants, and shoes. Erase the dotted lines.

#4

Add fingers, ears, and curly hair.

Draw your clown here. Give your clown two balloons.

Following Directions • 1–2   ©2004 Creative Teaching Press

Draw a Puppy

#1

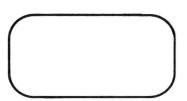

Draw the puppy's body.

#2

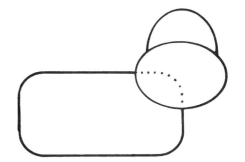

Add the face and head.
Erase the dotted line.

#3

Add the ears, a tail, legs, and feet.

#4

Draw eyes, a nose, and a mouth.
Add spots on the puppy's body.

Draw your puppy here. Draw a ball for your puppy to play with.

Draw a Flower

#1

#2

Draw a circle for the center of the flower.

Add four petals around the center.

#3

#4

Draw four more petals.

Add a stem and leaves.

Draw your flower here. Add more flowers to make a garden.

Following Directions • 1–2   ©2004 Creative Teaching Press

Name: _____

Draw a Fish

#1

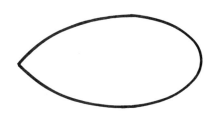

Draw the body of the fish.

#2

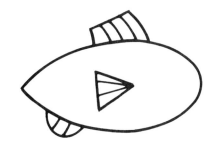

Add three fins.

#3

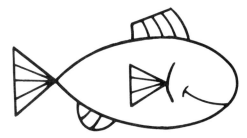

Add a tail, gill, and mouth.

#4

Draw eyes, scales, and bubbles.

Draw your fish here. Add sand, plants, and water for your fish.

Name: _____

Draw a Spider

#1

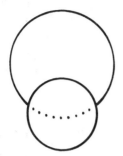

Draw two circles.
Erase the dotted line.

#2

Draw a circle for the head.
Erase the dotted line.

#3

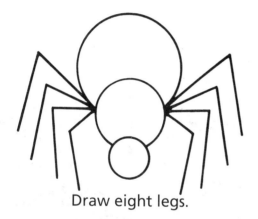

Draw eight legs.

#4

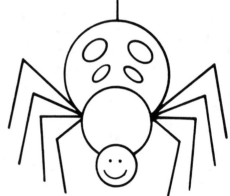

Add spots, eyes, a mouth,
and part of the spider's web.

Draw your spider here. Draw a fly buzzing around your spider.

Following Directions • 1–2 ©2004 Creative Teaching Press

Following Oral Directions

Oral Directions To Be Read by the Teacher

To the Teacher:

Be sure each student has the appropriate activity sheet and crayons. Ask students to listen very carefully, because you will read each direction only once. They are to listen and do only what you tell them to do. Read each step in the directions slowly and clearly. Pause long enough after each step to give students time to complete the steps you've read, but don't let the pace drag. Do not repeat any of the directions.

Page 48: What Are These Mammals Missing?

Draw a black tail on the horse.
Draw four orange stripes on the tiger's body.
Draw five brown spots on the giraffe's neck.
Draw a curly tail on the pig.
Draw a round black nose on the panda's face.
Draw six whiskers on the cat's face.

Page 49: Color a Cookie

On the first gingerbread cookie, color the vest red and the pants blue.
On the second gingerbread cookie, color the pants purple and the vest yellow.
On the third gingerbread cookie, color the vest green and the pants brown.
On the fourth gingerbread cookie, color the pants brown and the vest orange.
On the fifth gingerbread cookie, color the vest yellow and the pants red.
On the sixth gingerbread cookie, color the pants green and draw brown stripes on the vest.

Page 50: Plenty of Pets

Draw a bone for the puppy to chew.
Draw an orange carrot for the rabbit's dinner.
Draw a green plant in the fish's bowl.
Draw four green squares on the turtle's shell.
Draw a rock for the snake to crawl over.
Draw a bowl inside the cage for the hamster's food.

Page 51: Many Mice

Write the number 4 on the mouse resting on the log.
Write the number 2 on the mouse resting inside the log.
Write the number 5 on the mouse resting in front of the log.
Write the number 1 on the mouse resting outside the end of the log.
Write the number 6 on the mouse walking toward the log.
Write the number 3 on the mouse walking away from the log.

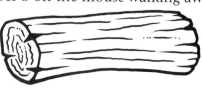

Following Directions • 1–2 ©2004 Creative Teaching Press

Oral Directions To Be Read by the Teacher

Page 52: What's for My Snack?

Color all the shapes with the letter **G** inside them **green**.
　Put your crayon down when you have finished.
Color all the shapes with the letter **B** inside them **brown**.
　Put your crayon down when you have finished.
Color all the shapes with the letter **R** inside them **red**.
　Put your crayon down when you have finished.
Color all the shapes with the letter **Y** inside them **yellow**.
　Put your crayon down when you have finished.

Page 53: Who's Hiding?

Color the shapes with the number **1** in them **yellow**.
Color the shapes with the number **2** in them **green**.
Color the shapes with the number **3** in them **red**.
Color the shapes with the number **4** in them **blue**.
Color the shapes with the number **5** in them **brown**.

Page 54: Mystery Insect

What is the mystery insect? To find out, you will draw lines on your paper from one letter to another as I name them: Start by finding letter A. Now draw a line from A to Q. Continue in this way as I call out letters one at a time. From Q go to: W, E, R, T, Y, U, I, O, P, S, D, F, G, B, H, N, J, M, K, L, Z, C, X, V, BB, and back to A. Color the mystery insect.

Page 55: Way to Go!

What is the mystery vehicle? To find out, you will draw lines on your paper from one number to another as I name them: Start by finding number 1. Now draw a line from 1 to 6. Continue in this way as I call out numbers one at a time. From 6 go to: 2, 5, 14, 8, 4, 12, 3, 10, 15, 19, 16, 7, 18, 23, 9, 11, 13, 17, 20, and back to 1. Color the mystery vehicle.

Page 56: Vowel Gumballs

Find the two gumballs with words that start with the vowel **A**. Color them **green**.
Find the two gumballs with words that start with the vowel **E**. Color them **yellow**.
Find the two gumballs with words that start with the vowel **I**. Color them **red**.
Find the two gumballs with words that start with the vowel **O**. Color them **blue**.
Find the two gumballs with words that start with the vowel **U**. Color them **purple**.

Oral Directions To Be Read by the Teacher

Page 57: Create a Creature

Color the first and last claws on the creature's feet red.
Color the middle claws blue on the creature's feet.
Color the first three teeth yellow. Color the last three teeth green.
Color the horn on the left purple.
Color the horn on the right orange.
Draw five circles on the creature's body.
Color the circles yellow.
Give your creature a name. Write its name on the line.

Page 58: Fishing Fun

Color fish #1 green. Draw a green line from this fish to Omar's fishing pole.
Color fish #2 orange. Draw an orange line from this fish to Manuel's fishing pole.
Color fish #3 red. Draw a red line from this fish to Juanita's fishing pole.
Color fish #4 purple. Draw a purple line from this fish to Karen's fishing pole.
Color fish #5 blue. Draw a blue line from this fish to Maya's fishing pole.
Color fish #6 brown. Draw a brown line from this fish to Ben's fishing pole.

Page 59: Find a Package

Find the package to the left of package number 6. Color it red.
Find the package directly above package number 7. Color it orange.
Find the package below package number 6. Draw three purple flowers on it.
Find the package to the right of package number 1. Draw brown stripes on it.
Find the package between package number 7 and package number 9. Draw three blue circles on it.
Find the package directly above package number 6. Color it green.
Find the package directly below package number 4. Color it yellow.
Find the package to the left of package number 2. Color it blue.
Find the package below package number 3. Draw two yellow stars on it.

Following Directions • 1–2 © 2004 Creative Teaching Press

Oral Directions To Be Read by the Teacher

Page 60: Match a Mutt

These six dogs have been separated from their owners. Help match them up by listening
and following directions.

Draw a line from Roxy to the girl wearing sandals. Color her shirt green.

Draw a line from Hershey to the boy wearing boots. Color his boots brown.

Draw a line from Jake to the girl who is sitting down. Color her shorts red.

Draw a line from Coco to the boy wearing a baseball cap. Color his cap blue.

Draw a line from Cleo to the girl with curly hair. Color her overalls purple.

Draw a line from Daisy to the boy holding a football. Color his football orange.

Page 61: Choose the Shoes

Put a number 1 on the shoe someone would wear to go to the beach. Color the shoe yellow.

Put a number 2 on the shoe someone would wear to go hiking. Color the shoe brown.

Put a number 3 on the shoe someone would wear to ballet class. Color the shoe pink.

Put a number 4 on the shoe someone would wear with his or her pajamas. Color the shoe green.

Put a number 5 on the shoe a cowboy would wear. Color the shoe black.

Put a number 6 on the shoe someone would wear to play basketball. Color the shoe red.

Page 62: Decorate the Cupcakes

Find cupcake number 5. Draw three red flowers on the top of this cupcake.

Find cupcake number 3. Write your first name in black on the top of this cupcake.

Find cupcake number 6. Draw three red squares on the top of this cupcake.

Find cupcake number 1. Draw two green circles on the top of this cupcake.

Find cupcake number 4. Draw four blue birthday candles on the top of this cupcake.

Find cupcake number 2. Draw two orange triangles on the top of this cupcake.

Page 63: House Hunting

Find the house made of bricks. Color the house red. Color
the roof black.

Find the house with a chimney. Color the house and roof
yellow. Color the chimney brown.

Find the house with the tile roof. Color the house and roof
brown. Do not color the windows.

Find the house with a wooden fence. Color the house and roof
blue. Color the fence brown.

Find the house with a cat in the window. Color the house and
roof orange. Color the cat black.

Find the house with a bird on the roof. Color the house and
roof green. Color the bird yellow.

What Are These Mammals Missing?

Color a Cookie

Plenty of Pets

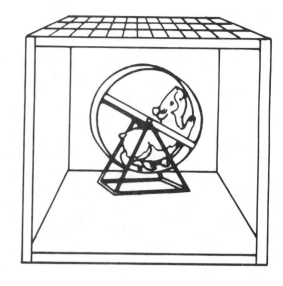

Following Directions • 1–2 ©2004 Creative Teaching Press

Name: _____

Many Mice

Name: _____

What's for My Snack?

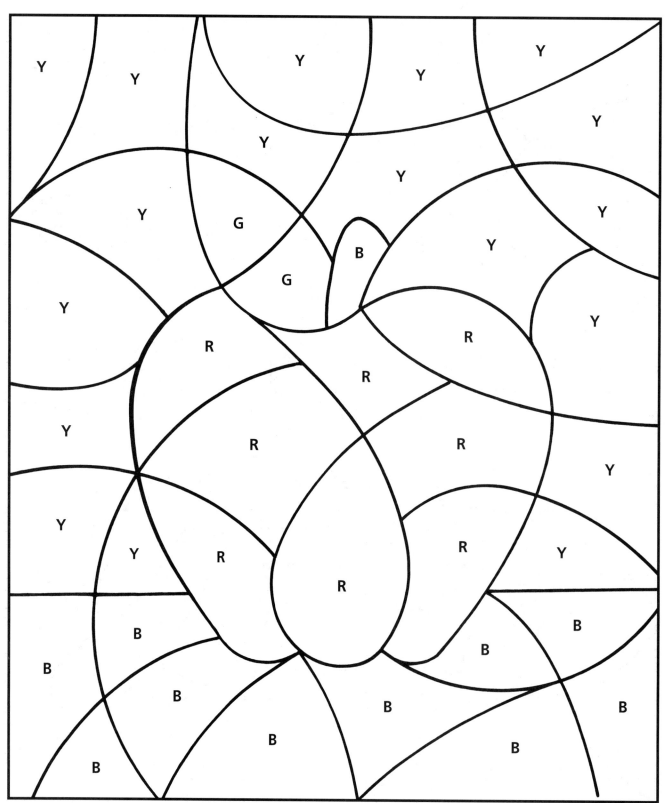

Following Directions • 1–2 ©2004 Creative Teaching Press

Name: _____

Who's Hiding?

Mystery Insect

Following Directions • 1–2 ©2004 Creative Teaching Press

Way to Go!

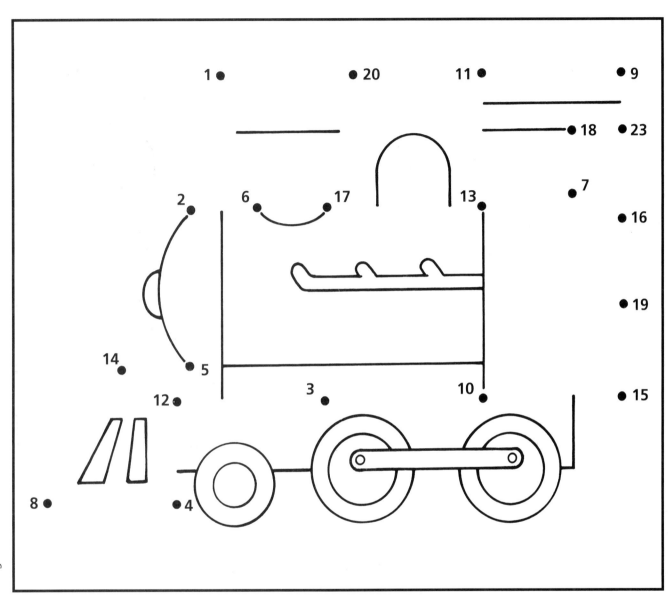

Vowel Gumballs

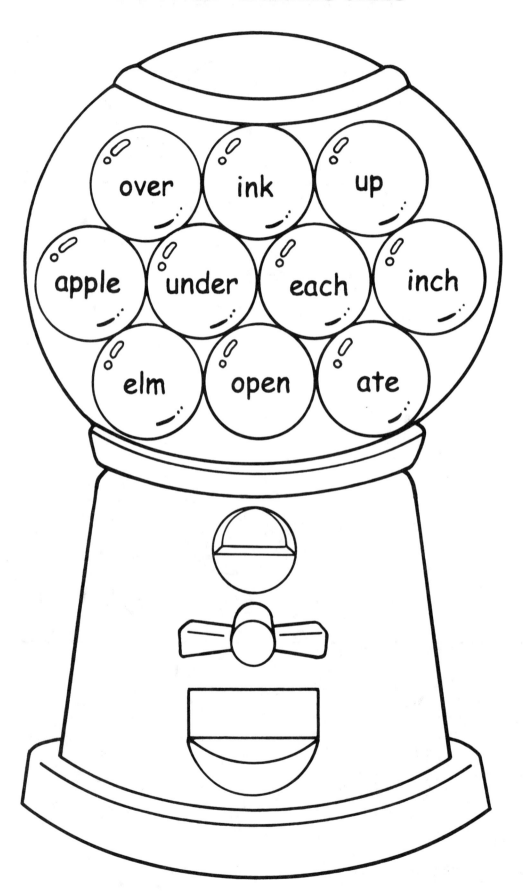

Following Directions • 1–2 ©2004 Creative Teaching Press

Name: _____

Create a Creature

My creature's name is _____ .

Name: _____

Fishing Fun

Following Directions • 1–2 ©2004 Creative Teaching Press

Find a Package

Name: _____

Match a Mutt

Daisy

Hershey

Jake

Coco

Roxy

Cleo

Following Directions • 1–2 ©2004 Creative Teaching Press

Choose the Shoes

Decorate the Cupcakes

Following Directions • 1–2   ©2004 Creative Teaching Press

House Hunting

Answer Key

Pages 14–15: Riddle Time #1

When you feed it, a little goes a long way.

Pages 16–17: Riddle Time #2

His trunk was too big to fit under the seat.

Page 28: Crack the Code

Have a happy day!

Page 52: What's for My Snack?

an apple

Page 53: Who's Hiding?

a parrot

Page 54: Mystery Insect

a butterfly

Page 55: Way to Go!

a train

FOLLOWING DIRECTIONS
AWARD

PRESENTED TO:

_____

_____
DATE

_____
TEACHER'S SIGNATURE

  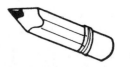